Brilliant Bob is Stoic

Written by
Kenneth T Jolivet

Copyright © 2021 by Kenneth T Jolivet
ISBN: 978-1-7365139-5-8
Edited by Melissa Peitsch
Illustrated by Renata Christine
Book Layout by Solaja Slobodan
All rights reserved

It was Saturday morning.

Brilliant Bob had a hard time sleeping last night.

He was too excited about what he was going to do today and over the weekend.

Brilliant Bob's dad was taking him and his friends—Dazzling Dave, Genuine George, and Superboy Sam—camping for two nights.

Bob got dressed quickly and hurried to the kitchen for breakfast.

"Good morning, Mom and Dad," Bob said, grinning with genuine love and excitement.

"What's for breakfast?"

Bob's dad had made a hearty breakfast of eggs, toast, bacon and hash browns.

They needed lots of energy for their weekend of camping and fun.

And this breakfast would do the trick.

You'd have thought there were goblins in the room because the food seemed to disappear as fast as it hit Bob's plate.

woosh

There was no need to hang around.
Time was precious.
"Let's go," said Bob's dad.
Bob's mom waved as the campers
drove off on their adventure.
It was a two-hour drive to the national park
where they'd all be camping.
The park had lots of trees, a river,
and plenty of wildlife.

They were going to play, explore, fish, eat around a campfire, and tell stories in the dark.
They'd packed some hot dogs and hamburgers to cook and marshmallows to roast over the campfire.
Brilliant Bob loved sticky, sweet, toasted marshmallows.
The four boys listened to music and played games while in the van to pass the time.
Finally, they'd arrived!

~ 7 ~

Incredibly, Bob's dad managed to find the perfect camping site.

It had a flat area for the tent, stones to create a fire pit, and wood stumps for seats.

First job was to set up the huge tent.

They were all going to sleep in one tent so Bob's dad could keep an eye on the four boys.

Brilliant Bob's dad gave each boy a job to do.

They worked together to spread out the large tarp, with a boy pulling at each corner.

Then the boys took turns helping with the tent poles and stakes, and finally, they set up the large tent on top of the tarp bottom.

With the biggest job done, and everything unpacked, it was time for some fun!

Dazzling Dave had brought his football and was ready to throw it.

Genuine George brought his fast legs: he planned on doing lots of running.

George also loved to play tag and hide and seek.

Man, it was always amazing to see how Dazzling Dave could throw that football.

He threw the perfect spiral just about every time and so very far.

And remarkably, Genuine George was so fast, he'd always get there to catch it.

Before they knew it, it was lunchtime,

The boys refueled with the sandwiches Brilliant Bob's mom had packed.

They ate quickly, because they were in a hurry to go fishing.

Bob's dad told them they were going to go to the river to catch some fish for their dinner.

Because this was an activity weekend, each boy had brought their own backpack to carry their own important things.

And they each had a small fishing pole that folded nicely for such occasions.

Off they went.

After about a half hour of walking through the forest to find the river, the sky began to grow dark and the wind began to blow in gusts.

They walked faster, hurrying to get to the river.

They wanted to catch their dinner before the storm would make it unsafe.

But they weren't exactly sure how to get to the river.

Bob's dad had a good map and a compass, but some of the landmarks and signposts on the trail were missing.

In their haste to beat the possible storm, they found themselves lost.

As fast, strong, smart, and agile as the boys were, none of these traits and abilities had prepared them for the unknown and the fear that went with it.

They were lost, worried and to be honest…scared.

The thunder was loud and the lightening was blinding and too close for comfort.

The four boys talked over each other as their imaginations began to run wild.

Brilliant Bob's dad could sense the boys beginning to panic.

He could see that they were close to tears.

It was time to lead and act.

Brilliant Bob's dad blew the whistle he'd packed.

This got the boys' attention real fast.

There was pure silence except for the howling wind and occasional thunder.

"Boys… it's time to pull ourselves together," Bob's dad said.

"In times like this, we must focus to control our minds and fears.

We must think logically with our heads.

We need courage and strength and common sense to guide us," he said.

"There's no use panicking and losing control of our emotions."

"It's time to be stoic.

That means enduring the fear and the hardship of being lost, and dealing with whatever comes our way without complaining," he explained.

"We stay composed."

He told the boys they needed to work together as a team, thinking clearly and logically.

"Of course it's scary," Bob's dad said, "but there's no time for fear now."

They needed to forget about fishing and get back to camp.

To do that, they would need to focus, using all their energy to get them there before dark.

Brilliant Bob's dad gave them instructions: it was best to keep everyone busy.

"Superboy Sam, you're going to keep an eye on the weather and keep us updated."

"Genuine George, you're going to carry this map and help us find our way."

"Dazzling Dave, you're going to listen very carefully. We don't want to run into any wild animals, and sounds of other people would mean safety."

"Brilliant Bob, you're going to help me clear the brush, so we can get through more easily."

Hours had passed since they had first set out to go fishing, and it was getting too dark for Bob's dad's liking.

Brilliant Bob's dad called the boys together and told them it was now too late to make it back to the camp.

They needed to use the remaining light to build their own shelter to spend the night in the woods.

"Okay boys, let's all stay within sight of each other and gather branches and twigs," he directed.

"We're going to make a tent with nature's gifts."

They soon gathered enough material to build a structure between some trees.

Their 'nature shelter' had a roof and three sides.

They left a large opening so they could see outside, and easily go in and out.

They were all very proud and excited in some strange way.

They were making the best of a bad situation.

Brilliant Bob said, "Wow, this is kind of fun!"

The other boys agreed as they each high-fived Bob's dad and each other.

The next job was to gather stones, kindling, and plenty of firewood.

They were going to make a fire to keep warm.

And this way, they could still sit around a fire and tell stories.

Bob's dad knew this would keep the boys' minds occupied.

Brilliant Bob had even brought a bag of marshmallows in his backpack! And so did Dazzling Dave.

Smartly, they'd all packed drinks and a few light snacks.

They'd missed out on their fish dinner, but they wouldn't starve.

Bob's dad had brought matches, and it didn't take long to light a fire.

Soon they were toasting the marshmallows on long twigs, and enjoying the sticky treats.

Before long, it was story time.

Each boy told stories in turn, as did Brilliant Bob's dad.

Some stories were silly and some were spooky.

Was there really such a thing as a Sasquatch?

The boys were having so much fun that they'd forgotten all about being lost.

And they weren't even cold, thanks to the fire.

It was getting late and Brilliant Bob's dad knew they'd have to get up early with the sunrise so they would have the best chance to get back to their camp during daylight.

Protectively, he announced it was time to get some sleep.

But because they were sleeping in the unsettled section of the forest, they would take turns keeping watch during the whole night.

Each boy would sit with Bob's dad for two hours over the course of the night.

They were in this together!

And this allowed each boy to help keep Bob's dad awake and look out for danger.

Brilliant Bob volunteered to take the first shift with his dad.

The others went to bed and fell asleep quickly.

It had been a long, difficult day and they were tired.

Two hours had passed.

It was Dazzling Dave's turn.

Another two hours later and it was Genuine George's turn to help guard the fort.

And lastly, it was Superboy Sam's turn.

Before they knew it, the sun was rising.

It was time to pack up and leave their homemade shelter.

The boys looked around at what they had made and were very proud.

They were also sad to leave it behind, but they couldn't wait to get back to camp.

Brilliant Bob's dad gathered the boys for a pep talk.

"Okay, everyone has the same job they had yesterday.

Any questions?

Let's get back to the tent!"

High fives all around!

Each boy was focused.

They used the sun's position through the trees to navigate.

They were making progress, but still weren't quite sure where to go.

They just knew to head south.

It was Dazzling Dave's job to listen for any sounds.

"Quiet," Dazzling Dave said. "I think I hear people!"

Sure enough, he did.

They all heard it.

Everyone stayed quiet so Brilliant Bob's dad could lead them to the source of the sounds.

Remarkably, they'd found their way back to camp!

They were all very happy and hugged each other in joy.

After getting settled again and while preparing lunch, they all admitted to feeling a little strange.

They weren't feeling as happy as they thought they'd be.

Yes, they were grateful to be back, but they each admitted to loving their adventure.

They'd been scared, they'd been lost, and they'd been hungry;

But... *somehow, they'd had fun!*

The stormy adventure helped the boys realize that being stoic helped them push away bad emotions and fear, which allowed them to focus.

Being stoic saved the day.

Not only that, it made it fun!

The boys couldn't wait to camp again that night.

Only this time, they stayed in the campsite and cooked the hot dogs and hamburgers they'd brought to eat.

And they looked forward to actually sleeping in their comfy sleeping bags.

The boys toasted each other with sodas around the campfire...

"Being stoic is cool!"

Brilliant Bob thanks you for reading this book.
He also invites you to join him in his other great adventures where:

Brilliant Bob is Competitive
Brilliant Bob is Strong
Brilliant Bob is Curious
Brilliant Bob Takes a Risk
Brilliant Bob is Brave
Brilliant Bob is Persistent

HIGH FIVE DUDE!

You can buy all seven books on Amazon.
And don't forget to visit Brilliant Bob's website at…

www.BrilliantBobKidBooks.com

CPSIA information can be obtained
at www.ICGtesting.com
Printed in the USA
BVHW022135220421
605705BV00007B/27